The Perfect Timing of Butterflies

By Phyllis Calvey
Illustrated by Jodi O'Grady

Have you ever thought about the stages of a butterfly? Its life begins as an egg, and it is born as a caterpillar. It explores the world around it, eating and growing, experiencing life. At the end of this stage, it seals itself inside of a chrysalis. What appears to be an end is really just the beginning. Miraculously, it emerges as something more beautiful than we could ever dream, free and no longer earthbound.

What a beautiful way to help us explain death to a child and to imagine with them our loved ones, not experiencing an ending but a miraculous beginning, something more beautiful than we could ever dream!

The Perfect Timing of Butterflies

Produced and printed by Stillwater River Publications.

Visit our website at **www.StillwaterPress.com** for more information.

First Stillwater River Publications Edition

ISBN: 978-1-968548-99-5 (paperback), 978-1-968548-98-8 (hardcover)

Library of Congress Control Number: 2026905700

1 2 3 4 5 6 7 8 9 10

Publisher's Cataloging-in-Publication
Provided by Cassidy Cataloguing Services, Inc.

Names: Calvey, Phyllis, author. | O'Grady, Jodi, illustrator.
Title: The perfect timing of butterflies / by Phyllis Calvey ; illustrated by Jodi O'Grady.
Description: First Stillwater River Publications edition. | West Warwick, RI, USA : Stillwater River Publications, [2026] | Interest age level: 008-010.
Identifiers: LCCN: 2026905700 | ISBN: 9781968548995 (paperback) | 9781968548988 (hardcover)
Subjects: LCSH: Butterflies—Juvenile fiction. | Death—Juvenile fiction. | Life cycles (Biology)—Juvenile fiction. | CYAC: Butterflies—Fiction. | Death—Fiction. | Life cycles—Fiction. | LCGFT: Fiction.
Classification: LCC: PZ7.1.C3235 Pe 2026 | DDC: [Fic]—dc23

Written by Phyllis Calvey.
Cover and illustrations by Jodi O'Grady.
Edited by Jodi O'Grady.

Published by Stillwater River Publications, West Warwick, RI, USA.

Author's Dedication

I want to thank the countless people who have taken the time to share their inspirational stories with me; they continue to enrich my life. To my children, grandchildren, and great grandchild, thank you for being such an integral part of the writing of this book. And especially, to my husband and Jessie, who never tired of doing yet one more reread. Your love sustains me.

Illustrator's Dedication

I want to thank my family for their love and support, especially Amam, for always believing that I can do anything. To my husband and children, thank you all for your patience and encouragement and for listening to me talk about this book incessantly for over three years. Thank you, Chloe and Magnolia, for being my second and third set of eyes on the text and illustrations. And thank you to all the special people in my life who have inspired my journey to seek God in all things!

Have you ever experienced a coincidence, an event that seems like it was planned, but it happened merely by chance? Maybe you were thinking about your favorite candy, and someone bought it for you as a surprise. Or you and a friend randomly wore the same shirt to school.

Sometimes, these things do happen by chance. But, when there is faith in God, so many experiences in your life no longer feel like a coincidence.

For decades, children and adults from across the country have shared stories with me that held a common theme: they received comfort they so desperately needed when a butterfly suddenly appeared at the same time they were missing someone who had died. It wasn't simply the sudden appearance of the butterfly that made it special; it was the perfect timing and their unshakable feeling that they had received a message from God. No one needed to make that connection for them. It was just something they felt deep inside.

I have chosen some of my favorite true stories to share with you. May you find peace as you read of God's love for us delivered in the perfect timing of butterflies.

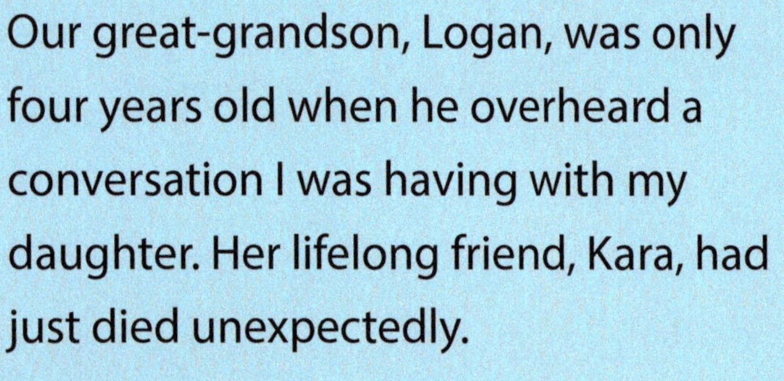

Our great-grandson, Logan, was only four years old when he overheard a conversation I was having with my daughter. Her lifelong friend, Kara, had just died unexpectedly.

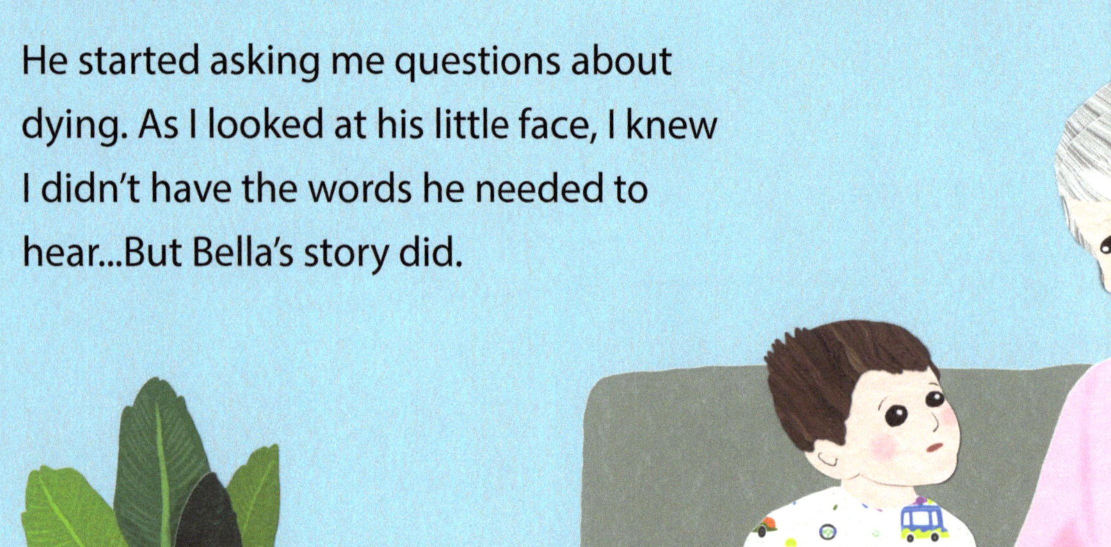

He started asking me questions about dying. As I looked at his little face, I knew I didn't have the words he needed to hear...But Bella's story did.

Bella's Story

Deputy Chief John McKee was a hero. To Bella, he was her Poppa. He was a policeman, and she knew he was often called to help people. Bella and her grandmother, Sandra, were so proud of him and the work he did. They knew his job was very important. Bella knew she was important to him too.

One day, a big disaster happened in New York City, and he was going to be away from home for a long time. It was always hard to say goodbye.

Years later, Bella's Poppa became very sick. Sandra told Bella that many people who had gone to help in New York with him were getting sick too.

They were both so sad when he died.

On the day of Poppa's funeral, Bella wanted to do something special for him. She remembered the day when they planted an apple tree together. She asked her grandmother if it would be alright to put an apple from that tree in her Poppa's casket to remember her by.

Her grandmother thought it was a wonderful idea.

As Bella was picking the apple and thinking about how much she missed her Poppa, a yellow butterfly suddenly appeared! The butterfly landed softly on her hand and stayed there for the longest time before flying away.

She smiled as she watched the butterfly flutter up into the sky. In that moment, the sadness she had been carrying turned into joy. She could hardly contain her excitement as she ran back to her house to tell her grandmother what had happened.

Bella knew in her heart the butterfly had come to deliver a loving message from God that her Poppa was okay and in heaven.

At the funeral, Bella and her grandmother were amazed by the number of police officers who attended to honor her Poppa's service and sacrifice. It made Bella feel happy to know that so many people loved her Poppa.

As they stood in front of his casket, a beautiful white butterfly passed by her, flew over his casket a few times, then encircled the officers. Bella grabbed her grandmother's hand with a knowing smile. God had sent her another message.

Now, every time Bella sees a butterfly, she smiles and thinks of her Poppa. She will always remember the special messages she received in the perfect timing of butterflies.

"So, Logan, what do you think?" I asked when I finished telling him Bella's story.

"I think I would pick a hammer for Grandpa to remember me by. We always make things together. And," he said, looking into my eyes, "I would pick a butterfly for you."

I gave him a big hug and knew the story had comforted him in just the way he needed. Stories have a way of doing that.

Sam loved to play baseball, and his mother was his biggest fan. After every game, they would get ice cream and talk about all the plays that he made. His mother was so proud and would leap from her seat when he got a hit or caught a high fly. She laughed and told him how, whenever a ball was hit toward him, she would hold her breath until it was safely in his glove.

Sam's Story

Sam knew his mother had been sick. Every day, he prayed that she would get better. Sadly, she became more tired as the days went by.

One night, she called him to her bedside and told him how much she loved him. She told him that she prayed too but that God doesn't always answer prayers in ways we can understand.

He climbed into bed next to her. As she held him tightly, she whispered, "Whenever you miss me, just close your eyes and think of my love for you. I promise you'll feel like I'm near."

Later that night, she passed away.

The day came for Sam to play in his first baseball game of the season without his mother, and it happened to be on Mother's Day weekend. He was missing her so much. He didn't know if he would be able to get through the game, but he loved his team and his coach and didn't want to let them down.

When it was his turn up to bat, his heart felt so broken. He couldn't help but look into the stands, even though he knew his mother wouldn't be there.

He saw Uncle Chris, who took care of him now and had been so good to him. He saw faces of friends and neighbors, who brought meals to them when his mother was too sick to cook. Others drove him to his practices and games to help out. He remembered how she told him that God sometimes works through people like that to show His love and presence in hard times.

Sam took a deep breath as he fought to hold back his tears.

Sam started to get ready for the first pitch. As he stepped up to the plate, from out of nowhere, a flurry of white butterflies surrounded him!

There was a shared feeling among everyone who knew Sam that these butterflies were no coincidence. The crowd began to cheer, and many of them cried tears of joy as the butterflies continued to swirl around him.

But Sam wasn't crying. In fact, he was wearing a big grin. He knew the butterflies carried a special message that his mother was safe in heaven.

He remembered what she told him on the night she died. He closed his eyes and thought about her love for him. He imagined her cheering for him, like she always had.

She was right! It felt as if she was right there with him.

Now, every time he sees a butterfly, he thinks of his mother and the special message God sent to him in the perfect timing of butterflies.

Billy's Story

Billy was a sweet boy who loved his teacher, Miss Jessie, and all his friends at his preschool. They always had so much fun learning and playing together.

One evening, Miss Jessie received a difficult phone call from the preschool letting her know that there had been a terrible accident. Billy had died.

The school also called the parents of Billy's friends to let them know the sad news. Nobody wanted to believe it was true, especially Billy's friends.

The day came for the preschool to open again. As Miss Jessie got ready for work that morning, she prayed that she would know how to comfort her students. She knew that close friends and family were gathering that morning to say goodbye to Billy at his funeral, and this first day back to school would be a hard day for all of them.

No one had been inside the school since the accident. Billy's clothes and stuffed animal were still in his cubby.

The children gathered around Miss Jessie and told her they felt sad. Miss Jessie decided to take the children outside to go for a walk. She told them that walking in fresh air helps her feel better when she is feeling sad.

As they started to walk around the school playground, one of Miss Jessie's students ran over and took her hand. The other students joined them, linking hands, as they continued to walk together. No one said a word, but they were all quietly thinking about their friend. They missed Billy.

Everyone suddenly came to a stop as a small, orange and black butterfly began to flutter around them. It flew in a tight pattern near them, close enough to touch, then landed at their feet.

The butterfly allowed Jazmin to pick it up. She gently cupped it in her hands and then carefully let it go.

The butterfly flew high into the sky. It felt as if it was guiding their eyes toward where Billy had gone, and they all knew he was in heaven. They felt their sadness lift as they waved goodbye.

Now, every time they see a butterfly, they think of Billy. They will always remember the special moment they shared together and the message they received in God's perfect timing of the butterfly.

AnneMarie's Story

Sometimes, through sickness, heroes are made.

AnneMarie was an amazing young woman who bravely fought a disease called leukemia, a type of cancer that hurts blood cells. Her parents, Bob and Linda, were so proud and amazed as she overcame her shyness to teach people about the disease and the special way they could help.

AnneMarie taught people that everyone has special tissue in their bodies called bone marrow, and doctors can take small amounts of their healthy bone marrow to help cure people with leukemia. Because of her work, many children and adults were cured! She was a hero, and the people who donated their bone marrow to help became heroes too.

It brought AnneMarie so much joy to be able to help people get better, and everyone hoped that AnneMarie would be made well again too. Sadly, she became very ill with another sickness in her lungs. She noticed her body feeling weaker, and days became more difficult.

One day, as she sat with her father, she began to cry. She told him that she was afraid to die. He wanted so badly to take the sickness from her. He could see how tired she was as he held her close.

The next day, Bob sat by AnneMarie's bedside and handed her a beautiful snow globe with two butterflies inside.

"Don't be afraid," he whispered. "Like these butterflies, you'll never be alone."

It wasn't much later that AnneMarie died, peacefully at home. Bob knew his beautiful daughter was finally free from her sickness and no longer suffering. Still, missing her was sometimes so hard to bear. It was on those truly difficult days when butterflies would suddenly appear.

One day, Bob was taking a walk after he participated in The Cancer March on Washington. He was surprised by a large monarch that seemed to be floating on the breeze in front of him as if to say, "Hello!"

Moments later, he was greeted by a second, delicately painted butterfly, and he felt such great comfort. Simply being greeted by two butterflies in this way might seem like a small thing, but once God communicates with you in a particular way, it feels exactly like a hug from heaven each time it happens.

When he saw the third butterfly, he knew it was no coincidence. Now, every time he sees a butterfly, he remembers the message he received that day. God had chosen the perfect timing of butterflies to let him know his daughter was not alone. She was safe and in heaven with Him.

Rose's Story

Every October, for many years, my husband, Brian, and I have stayed at a little cottage on Peaks Island in Maine. On one particular trip, we were feeling very sad because his mother, Rose, had just died.

As we took our usual walk around the island, I thought about the time when I told Rose all about the butterfly stories I collected from people around the country. She had never heard stories like these before and kept repeating over and over, "You mean to tell me that butterflies come to comfort people after a loved one dies?" She just couldn't believe it.

Brian and I continued walking, feeling so brokenhearted when, all of a sudden, we saw the most unbelievable sight!

Monarch butterflies were everywhere! They covered the bushes and flowers and flew up in the air, coloring everything with their vibrant orange and black wings. My heart was so full of heaven's joy as they danced all around us! I felt the butterflies gently touching my arms, and we laughed when one even landed on my head! I couldn't help but join their dance, twirling and throwing my arms out, pretending like I was flying too.

I soon learned we had just experienced the beginning of a butterfly migration. What made it even much more special is that it was the only one we had ever been a part of in the nearly 30 years we had stayed on the island!

How beautiful is it that God didn't send us just one but a whole migration of butterflies, like the stories He sends me? It was so personal and perfectly timed that it was an undeniable message being lovingly conveyed to us that Rose was safe and in heaven. We were delighted that she now had her very own butterfly story, and so did we!

While not everyone will receive a message through the visit of a butterfly, that doesn't mean you won't have special stories of your own. God always knows when and where we need Him. And He knows how to speak to us in a way we can understand, a specific way, personal to us, that reminds us of our loved ones and brings us peace. Can you think of something that reminds you of your loved ones? Perhaps it's a special song, an animal, a pleasant smell, or maybe a book?

For Logan, as I shared with him about Bella and her butterflies, I watched his fears and worries fade away, and I realized they became a part of his story. And now, those butterflies can continue their flight to carry God's message of His hope and comfort to others through the pages of this book.

If you are missing someone special, I hope this book speaks to your heart and brings you healing. And maybe, just maybe, it found its way to you at the exact moment when you needed it most, just like in the perfect timing of butterflies.

Deputy Chief John P. McKee

Bella's Poppa courageously answered the call to assist with search, rescue, and recovery efforts at the World Trade Center on September 11, 2001. Having spent over a month at ground zero, he later developed cancer as a result of his exposure to the toxic materials at the site. John was only 49 years old when he died. He, along with many other heroes, sacrificed their lives during and following that tragic event, and our hearts go out to their families who made that ultimate sacrifice with them.

We would like to offer a special thank you to all of our country's first responders, service men and women, and all those who risk their lives every day to keep our Nation safe. And thank you to all the families who sacrifice time, peace, and sometimes so much more to support these brave efforts. May God bless you and keep you all.

Author and Illustrator Biography

Phyllis Calvey is an author, educator, speaker, and storyteller. More than a decade ago, butterflies captured her imagination and heart through the incredible true stories people have shared with her. Her deep love for them is felt in her writing, and her literary art on the topic of grieving continues to restore hope for so many people.

Please take a moment to visit her website, at www.butterflyclubbook.com, where you can read more butterfly stories and view her previously published works.

Phyllis and her husband Brian live in Bellingham, Massachusetts, surrounded by her dear family and bountiful garden.

Jodi O'Grady started writing and illustrating her own stories in the third grade. She studied graphic design and used her skills for close to twenty years in the government sector. While she enjoyed her professional career, this book is a dream come true, many years in the making.

Jodi is a homeschooling mom, teacher, and women's ministry leader. She lives in Massachusetts with her husband Kevin, their two children, and her sweet, furry doggy.

www.ingramcontent.com/pod-product-compliance
Lightning Source LLC
LaVergne TN
LVHW070201110826
845147LV00002B/466

9781968548995